contents

Please note that Australian cup and spoon measurements are metric.
A conversion chart appears on page 62.

lunchbox tips

A school lunchbreak should be something to look forward to. It should be a lovely surprise when your child opens their lunchbox – like having a picnic. Use baking paper to wrap sandwiches or wraps, and always keep them cool in the lunchbox with a freezer brick or frozen drink. Fruit should be chilled too – warm fruit is never nice.

Prepare salads in airtight plastic containers – if there's a dressing, pack it in a separate container – this prevents the salad from becoming soggy and also gives the lunch a picnic feel. Many of the recipes in this book can be fully or partially prepared the night before. Don't forget to freeze the drink or freezer brick to keep lunches cool.

Tips for working mothers

• Work out your children's school lunch menus for the week. Planning saves time, money, arguments and frustration.

• Make sure you have a range of different-sized airtight plastic containers for dressings and other accompaniments.

• Shop for the whole week's lunches in one go, if possible.

• Freeze all the drinks so they will keep the food in the lunchbox cool and will have thawed by lunchtime.

• Make sandwich fillings on the weekend or the night before and store in the fridge.

• Buy sliced bread or bread rolls and freeze. Remove from the freezer as soon as you get up in the morning – you should be able to cut them within half an hour.

• When preparing the family's dinner, think about leftovers – fried rice for example, or potato tortilla are both delicious cold the next day. Many children enjoy cold rice pudding, too.

• Chilled chopped fruit in a small container, along with a spoon, is often more appealing to children than a whole apple or pear.

• Keep clear of biscuits, muesli bars and other so-called "healthy" treats. Most of them are loaded with sugar and/or fat.

• Prepare vegetable sticks the night before and add a little container of dip – hummus or baba ghanoush are great.

fried brown rice

2 teaspoons vegetable oil
2 eggs, beaten lightly
2 rindless bacon rashers (130g), chopped finely
½ cup (75g) frozen peas
½ cup (80g) frozen corn kernels
250g packet pre-cooked brown rice
2 green onions, chopped finely
2 teaspoons soy sauce
1 tablespoon sweet chilli sauce, optional

1 Heat half the oil in large wok, add egg; swirl wok to make a thin omelette. Remove omelette from wok; roll and cut into thin strips.
2 Heat remaining oil in wok, add bacon; stir-fry until browned and crisp. Add peas and corn to wok; stir-fry until hot. Add rice, onion and soy sauce; stir-fry until combined. Cool.
3 Pack fried rice in lunchbox, top with omelette; refrigerate. Place sweet chilli sauce in separate airtight plastic container. The next day, pack lunchbox and sauce with a freezer brick or frozen drink. Just before eating, drizzle with sweet chilli sauce.

preparation time 10 minutes
cooking time 10 minutes
serves 2
nutritional count per serving 18g total fat (4.9g saturated fat); 2015kJ (482 cal); 52.9g carbohydrate; 23.8g protein; 6.1g fibre

tip The rice is best cooked a day before making this recipe. Spread evenly onto a tray and refrigerate overnight. **the night before** Make the fried rice; it must be completely cold before packing in a lunchbox.

the night before
Prepare the salad
and keep, covered,
in the refrigerator.

chicken pasta salad

¾ cup farfalle pasta
10g butter
1 clove garlic, crushed
50g button mushrooms, sliced thinly
1 small red capsicum (150g), chopped finely
2 teaspoons red wine vinegar
1 teaspoon wholegrain mustard
½ cup (80g) shredded barbecued chicken
1 tablespoon finely chopped fresh chives

1   Boil pasta in medium saucepan of boiling water until tender; drain.
Rinse pasta under cold water; drain well.
2   Melt butter in small frying pan, add garlic, mushrooms and capsicum;
cook, stirring, until vegetables are tender.
3   Shake vinegar and mustard together in small screw-top jar.
4   Combine pasta and vegetable mixture in medium bowl with chicken
and chives; cool
5   Pack salad in lunchbox; refrigerate. Place dressing in separate airtight
plastic container; refrigerate. The next day, pack lunchbox and dressing with
a freezer brick or frozen drink. Just before eating, drizzle salad with dressing.

preparation time 10 minutes
cooking time 10 minutes
serves 1
nutritional count per serving 16.9g total fat (7.4g saturated fat);
5008kJ (1198 cal); 198g carbohydrate; 53.9g protein; 13.1g fibre
tip Farfalle is a bow-tie shaped short pasta that is sometimes known
as butterfly pasta.

pasta salad

250g small pasta
⅔ cup (200g) mayonnaise
2 teaspoons wholegrain mustard
300g can butter beans, rinsed, drained
100g roasted capsicum, drained, chopped coarsely
250g cherry tomatoes, halved
100g leg ham, chopped coarsely
½ cup (55g) coarsely chopped baby green beans
⅓ cup (25g) parmesan cheese flakes

1 Cook pasta in large saucepan of boiling water until just tender; drain. Rinse pasta under cold water; drain well.
2 Transfer pasta to a large bowl, cool, then add combined mayonnaise and mustard to pasta. Stir in remaining ingredients.
3 Pack salad in lunchbox; refrigerate. The next day, pack lunchbox with a freezer brick or frozen drink.

preparation time 15 minutes
cooking time 10 minutes
serves 4
nutritional count per serving 21.7g total fat (3.7g saturated fat); 2073kJ (496 cal); 55.8g carbohydrate; 16.7g protein; 4.7g fibre

tip For extra fibre, use wholemeal pasta. For those who are gluten-intolerant, try gluten-free pasta.
the night before Prepare the salad and keep, covered, in the refrigerator.

the night before
Prepare the salad
and keep, covered,
in the refrigerator.

teriyaki chicken rice salad

¼ cup (50g) koshihikari rice
¼ cup (60ml) water
1 tablespoon rice vinegar
2 teaspoons teriyaki sauce
1cm piece fresh ginger (5g), grated
½ cup (80g) shredded barbecued chicken
½ lebanese cucumber (65g), seeded, chopped coarsely
1 small carrot (70g), grated coarsely
2 teaspoons toasted sesame seeds
¼ sheet toasted seaweed (yaki-nori), shredded

1 Rinse rice in cold water until water is almost clear; drain. Place rice and the water in small saucepan, cover; bring to the boil. Reduce heat; simmer, covered, about 10 minutes. Remove from heat; stand rice, covered, until cool.
2 Combine rice with vinegar, sauce and ginger in medium bowl. Add chicken, cucumber, carrot and 1 teaspoon sesame seeds; mix well.
3 Pack salad in lunchbox; refrigerate. The next day, sprinkle salad with seaweed and remaining sesame seeds. Pack lunchbox with a freezer brick or frozen drink.

preparation time 15 minutes
cooking time 10 minutes (plus standing time)
serves 1
nutritional count per serving 7.7g total fat (1.8g saturated fat); 1538kJ (368 cal); 47.8g carbohydrate; 23.7g protein; 5g fibre
tips Koshihikari is a small, round-grain white rice grown in Australia from Japanese seed. If unavailable, substitute a white short-grain rice such as arborio.
Toasted seaweed, also known as yaki-nori, is a type of dried seaweed used in Japanese cooking as a flavouring, garnish or for sushi. It is sold in thin sheets from supermarkets and Asian food stores.

blt salad

8 rindless bacon rashers (240g)
16 grape tomatoes, halved
1 medium cos lettuce
½ cup (40g) parmesan cheese flakes
mayonnaise dressing
⅓ cup (100g) mayonnaise
2 tablespoons hot water

1 Cook bacon in large frying pan until crisp; drain on absorbent paper. Chop coarsely.
2 Make mayonnaise dressing.
3 Combine bacon, tomato, lettuce and cheese in large bowl; toss gently.
4 Pack salad in lunchbox; refrigerate. Place dressing in separate airtight plastic container; refrigerate. The next day, pack lunchbox and dressing with a freezer brick or frozen drink. Just before eating, drizzle salad with dressing.
mayonnaise dressing Stir ingredients in a small jug until smooth.

preparation time 5 minutes
cooking time 10 minutes
serves 4
nutritional count per serving 19.8g total fat (6g saturated fat); 1254kJ (300 cal); 9.8g carbohydrate; 18.5g protein; 5g fibre

the night before
Prepare the salad and the
dressing and keep, covered,
in separate containers, in
the refrigerator.

the night before
Prepare the salad
and keep, covered,
in the refrigerator.

traffic light pasta salad

250g small pasta
1 small green capsicum (150g), chopped coarsely
250g cherry tomatoes
100g roast turkey breast or leg ham, chopped coarsely
125g cheddar cheese, cubed
2 tablespoons finely chopped chives
¼ cup (60ml) bottled french salad dressing

1 Cook pasta in large pan of boiling water until just tender; drain.
Rinse pasta under cold water; drain well. Transfer to a large bowl; cool.
2 Add remaining ingredients to pasta; toss to combine.
3 Pack salad in lunchbox; refrigerate. The next day, pack lunchbox with
a freezer brick or frozen drink.

preparation time 15 minutes
cooking time 10 minutes
serves 4
nutritional count per serving 12.7g total fat (7.1g saturated fat);
1651kJ (395 cal); 45g carbohydrate; 23.1g protein; 3.4g fibre

thai beef noodle salad

150g beef rump steak
20g bean thread noodles
¼ lebanese cucumber (30g), seeded, sliced
25g cherry tomatoes, halved
¼ small red capsicum (40g), sliced thinly
1 green onion, sliced thinly
dressing
¼ cup loosely packed fresh mint leaves
2 teaspoons peanut oil
2 teaspoons sweet chilli sauce
2 teaspoons lime juice

1 Cook beef in heated oiled small frying pan until cooked through.
Cover, stand 10 minutes then slice thinly.
2 Place noodles in medium heatproof bowl, cover with boiling water;
stand until tender, drain. Cut noodles into random lengths.
3 Combine beef and noodles in same bowl with cucumber, tomato,
capsicum and onion. Cool.
4 Make dressing.
5 Pack salad in lunchbox; refrigerate. Place dressing in separate
airtight plastic container; refrigerate. The next day, pack lunchbox
and dressing with a freezer brick or frozen drink. Just before eating,
drizzle salad with dressing.
dressing Combine ingredients in screw-top jar; shake well.

preparation time 15 minutes
cooking time 5 minutes
serves 1
nutritional count per serving 22.8g total fat (7.9g saturated fat);
1768kJ (423 cal); 16.2g carbohydrate; 36.8g protein; 3.1g fibre

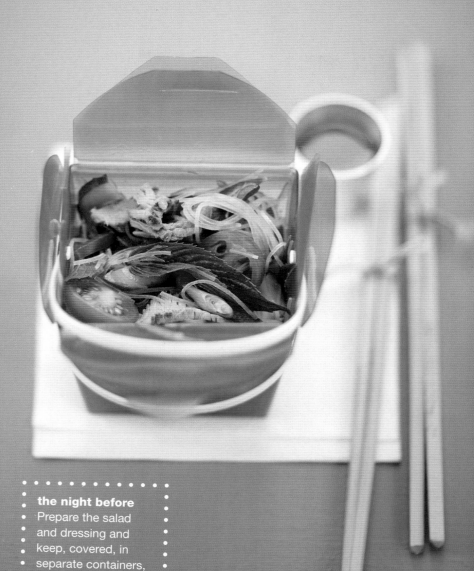

the night before
Prepare the salad
and dressing and
keep, covered, in
separate containers,
in the refrigerator.

the night before
Prepare the salad
and keep, covered,
in the refrigerator.

salmon pasta salad

1 cup (150g) spiral pasta
170g asparagus, trimmed, chopped coarsely
2 tablespoons low-fat ricotta cheese
1 teaspoon finely grated lemon rind
¼ cup (60ml) lemon juice
1 clove garlic, crushed
1 small red capsicum (150g), sliced thinly
⅓ cup coarsely chopped fresh flat-leaf parsley
2 green onions, sliced thinly
210g can pink salmon in springwater, drained, flaked

1 Cook pasta in medium saucepan of boiling water, uncovered, until just tender. Add asparagus; cook 1 minute. Drain. Rinse pasta and asparagus under cold water; drain well. Cool.
2 Combine cheese, rind, juice and garlic in large bowl; add pasta, asparagus and remaining ingredients to bowl; toss to combine.
3 Pack salad in lunchbox; refrigerate. The next day, pack lunchbox with a freezer brick or frozen drink.

preparation time 10 minutes
cooking time 10 minutes
serves 2
nutritional count per serving 8.5g total fat (2.9g saturated fat); 1860kJ (445 cal); 56.4g carbohydrate; 32.3g protein; 5.1g fibre

salads

niçoise salad

100g baby new potatoes, quartered
50g green beans, halved
95g can tuna in springwater, drained, flaked
25g cherry tomatoes, quartered
1 hard-boiled egg, quartered
1 tablespoon seeded black olives, chopped coarsely
1 tablespoon coarsely chopped fresh flat-leaf parsley
lemon slice

1 Cook potato and beans, separately, until tender. Rinse under cold water; drain. Cool.
2 Combine potato and beans with tuna, tomato, egg, olives and parsley in medium bowl.
3 Pack salad in lunchbox; refrigerate. The next day, pack lunchbox and lemon slice with a freezer brick or frozen drink.

preparation time 15 minutes
cooking time 10 minutes
serves 1
nutritional count per serving 7.8g total fat (2.4g saturated fat); 1179kJ (282 cal); 20.3g carbohydrate; 29.7g protein; 4.9g fibre

the night before
Prepare the salad
and keep, covered,
in the refrigerator.

tip You need ⅛ small wombok and ⅛ small red cabbage. Use leftover roast pork or chinese barbecued pork. **the night before** Prepare the salad and dressing; keep, covered, in separate containers in the refrigerator.

pork & cabbage salad

1 small carrot (70g)
¾ cup (60g) finely shredded wombok
¾ cup (60g) finely shredded red cabbage
1 green onion, sliced thinly
½ cup shredded leftover cooked pork
dressing
1 tablespoon olive oil
2 teaspoons cider vinegar
½ teaspoon dijon mustard

1 Make dressing.
2 Using a vegetable peeler, slice carrot into ribbons. Combine carrot in medium bowl with wombok, cabbage, onion and pork.
3 Pack salad in lunchbox; refrigerate. Place dressing in separate airtight plastic container; refrigerate. The next day, pack lunchbox and dressing with a freezer brick or frozen drink. Just before eating, drizzle salad with dressing.
dressing Combine ingredients in screw-top jar; shake well.

preparation time 20 minutes
serves 1
nutritional count per serving 21.2g total fat (3.6g saturated fat); 1436kJ (342 cal); 8.8g carbohydrate; 26.2g protein; 6.9g fibre

dijon chicken & salad wrap

200g chicken breast fillet
cooking-oil spray
1 tablespoon skim-milk natural yogurt
1 teaspoon dijon mustard
2 rye mountain bread wraps (60g)
20g baby spinach leaves
1 small tomato (90g), sliced thinly
1 small carrot (70g), grated coarsely

1 Spray chicken with cooking oil; cook chicken in heated small frying pan. Cool; shred coarsely. Combine chicken in medium bowl with yogurt and mustard; cover with plastic wrap, refrigerate.
2 The next day, divide chicken mixture between wraps; top with remaining ingredients. Roll up tightly to enclose filling; cut if half, if required. Wrap in baking paper or plastic wrap.
3 Pack wrap in lunchbox with a freezer brick or frozen drink.

preparation time 10 minutes
cooking time 15 minutes
makes 2
nutritional count per wrap 3.8g total fat (0.7g saturated fat); 932kJ (223 cal); 17.9g carbohydrate; 27.4g protein; 3.2g fibre

tips You can use any leafy greens you like in place of the spinach. You can also use barbecued chicken. **the night before** Cook the chicken and keep, covered, in the refrigerator. Prepare the wrap in the morning.

the night before
The wrap is best
made in the morning.

ricotta, basil & ham wrap

2 small zucchini (180g)
¼ cup (60g) low-fat ricotta cheese
3 rye mountain bread wraps (90g)
75g shaved ham
¼ cup coarsely chopped fresh basil

1 Using a vegetable peeler, slice zucchini lengthways into ribbons.
2 Divide cheese among wraps; top with zucchini, ham and basil. Roll up
tightly to enclose filling; cut in half. Wrap in baking paper or plastic wrap.
3 Pack wrap in lunchbox with a freezer brick or frozen drink.

preparation time 5 minutes
serves 2
nutritional count per serving 4.7g total fat (2.3g saturated fat);
886kJ (212 cal); 24.1g carbohydrate; 16.1g protein; 3.7g fibre

turkey & cranberry wrap

2 rye mountain bread wraps (60g)
2 tablespoons cranberry sauce
80g shaved turkey
30g snow pea sprouts
30g baby spinach leaves

1   Spread wraps with sauce; top with remaining ingredients. Roll up tightly to enclose filling; cut in half, if required. Wrap in baking paper or plastic wrap.

2   Pack wrap in lunchbox with a freezer brick or frozen drink.

preparation time 5 minutes
makes 2
nutritional count per wrap   2.1g total fat (0.4g saturated fat); 849kJ (203 cal); 27.6g carbohydrate; 16.7g protein; 2.5g fibre

tips Snow pea sprouts
are often hard to get.
Substitute with regular
bean sprouts or any other
kind you like. Use rocket
or any leftover greens
instead of the spinach.
the night before
The wrap is best made
in the morning.

the night before
The wrap is best
made in the morning.

tuna & sweet corn wrap

185g can tuna in springwater, drained
125g can corn kernels, drained
1 tablespoon mayonnaise
2 wholemeal lavash (120g)
½ small avocado (100g)
30g baby spinach leaves

1 Flake tuna into a medium bowl; stir in corn and mayonnaise.
2 Spread half of each lavash with avocado. Spread tuna mixture over avocado, then top with spinach. Roll lavash up tightly to enclose filling; cut in half, if required. Wrap in baking paper or plastic wrap.
3 Pack wrap in lunchbox with a freezer brick or frozen drink.

preparation time 5 minutes
makes 2
nutritional count per wrap 14.8g total fat (3.1g saturated fat); 1722kJ (412 cal); 40.1g carbohydrate; 26.2g protein; 6.4g fibre

wraps

guacamole & ham wrap

2 medium avocados (500g)
1 tablespoon lime juice
1 small tomato (90g), seeded, chopped finely
1 tablespoon finely chopped fresh chives
130g can corn kernels, drained
4 pieces lavash bread (240g)
200g shaved ham

1 Mash avocados with juice in small bowl. Stir in tomato, chives and corn.
2 Spread lavash with guacamole; top with ham. Roll up tightly to enclose filling; cut in half, if required. Wrap in baking paper or plastic wrap.
3 Pack wrap in lunchbox with a freezer brick or frozen drink.

preparation time 10 minutes
makes 4
nutritional count per wrap 23.2g total fat (5.2g saturated fat); 1877kJ (449 cal); 40.1g carbohydrate; 17.9g protein; 4.7g fibre

the night before
Boil the eggs. Make the
filling and the sandwiches
in the morning.

egg salad sandwich

6 hard-boiled eggs, chopped finely
1 stalk celery (150g), trimmed, chopped finely
1 green onion, sliced thinly
2 tablespoons finely grated parmesan cheese
¼ cup (75g) low-fat mayonnaise
1 cup (60g) shredded iceberg lettuce
2 large egg tomatoes (180g), sliced
8 slices white bread (360g)

1 Combine egg, celery, onion, cheese and mayonnaise in medium bowl.
2 Sandwich egg mixture, lettuce and tomato between bread slices; cut as desired. Wrap in baking paper or plastic wrap.
3 Pack sandwich in lunchbox with a freezer brick or frozen drink.

preparation time 15 minutes
makes 4
nutritional count per sandwich 13.6g total fat (4g saturated fat); 1622kJ (388 cal); 44.8g carbohydrate; 19.5g protein; 3.7g fibre

egg & chive sandwich

2 hard-boiled eggs, halved
1 tablespoon low-fat ricotta cheese
2 tablespoons low-fat cottage cheese
2 tablespoons finely chopped fresh chives
4 slices rye bread (180g)

1 Place egg, cheeses and chives in medium bowl; using potato masher or back of fork, mash until combined. Cover with plastic wrap, refrigerate.
2 Sandwich egg mixture between bread slices; cut as desired. Wrap in baking paper or plastic wrap.
3 Pack sandwich in lunchbox with a freezer brick or frozen drink.

preparation time 5 minutes
makes 2
nutritional count per sandwich 8.5g total fat (2.6g saturated fat); 1375kJ (329 cal); 40.6g carbohydrate; 19.2g protein; 6.2g fibre

the night before
Boil the eggs and make the filling; keep, covered in the refrigerator. Make the sandwiches in the morning. If you like, add some curry powder to the filling.

the night before
Make the filling and keep, covered, in the refrigerator. Make the sandwiches in the morning.

cheese & salad sandwich

200g low-fat cottage cheese
⅓ cup (40g) coarsely grated reduced-fat cheddar cheese
1 cup shredded baby spinach leaves
1 green onion, sliced thinly
1 small carrot (70g), grated finely
1 tablespoon toasted sesame seeds
2 teaspoons lemon juice
30g mesclun
8 slices of wholemeal bread (360g)

1 Combine cheeses, spinach, onion, carrot, sesame seeds and juice in medium bowl; cover with plastic wrap, refrigerate.
2 The next day, sandwich mesclun and cheese mixture between bread slices; cut as desired. Wrap in baking paper or plastic wrap.
3 Pack sandwich in lunchbox with a freezer brick or frozen drink.

preparation time 15 minutes
makes 4
nutritional count per sandwich 6g total fat (2.3g saturated fat); 911kJ (218 cal); 20.9g carbohydrate; 17.5g protein; 4.5g fibre

tuna, celery
& dill sandwich

185g can tuna in springwater, drained, flaked
2 stalks celery (300g), trimmed, chopped finely
¼ small red onion (25g), chopped finely
2 tablespoons low-fat ricotta cheese
1 tablespoon coarsely chopped fresh dill
2 teaspoons rinsed, drained baby capers
20g baby spinach leaves
4 slices rye bread (180g)

1 Combine tuna, celery, onion, cheese, dill and capers in medium
bowl; cover with plastic wrap, refrigerate.
2 The next day, sandwich spinach and tuna mixture between bread slices;
cut as desired. Wrap in baking paper or plastic wrap.
3 Pack sandwich in lunchbox with a freezer brick or frozen drink.

preparation time 10 minutes
makes 2
nutritional count per sandwich 6g total fat (2.2g saturated fat);
1517kJ (363 cal); 42.5g carbohydrate; 29.9g protein; 8.4g fibre

tip The spinach (or try cos lettuce) will stop the bread from turning soggy. **the night before** Make the filling and keep, covered, in the refrigerator. Make the sandwiches in the morning.

the night before
This sandwich is best
made in the morning.

chicken, celery
& avocado sandwich

⅓ cup (50g) finely shredded cooked chicken
1 stalk celery (150g), trimmed, chopped finely
¼ small avocado (50g)
1 teaspoon lemon juice
2 slices white sandwich bread (90g)

1 Combine chicken, celery, avocado and juice in small bowl.
2 Sandwich chicken mixture between bread slices; cut as desired.
Wrap in baking paper or plastic wrap.
3 Pack sandwich in lunchbox with a freezer brick or frozen drink.

preparation time 10 minutes
makes 1
nutritional count per sandwich 13.2g total fat (3g saturated fat);
1354kJ (324 cal); 30.1g carbohydrate; 19g protein; 4.2g fibre

beef, cheese
& carrot sandwich

½ small carrot (35g), grated coarsely
2 tablespoons spreadable cream cheese
2 tablespoons finely shredded iceberg lettuce
2 slices white sandwich bread (90g)
¼ cup finely chopped roast beef

1 Combine carrot, cream cheese and lettuce in small bowl.
2 Sandwich beef and carrot mixture between bread slices; cut
as desired. Wrap in baking paper or plastic wrap.
3 Pack sandwich in lunchbox with a freezer brick or frozen drink.

preparation time 10 minutes
makes 1
nutritional count per sandwich 16.7g total fat (9.3g saturated fat);
1701kJ (407 cal); 43g carbohydrate; 19.1g protein; 3.9g fibre

the night before
This sandwich is best
made in the morning.

the night before
The pockets are best
made in the morning.

roast beef & slaw pockets

2 cups (160g) finely shredded cabbage
1 small red onion (100g), chopped finely
1 small carrot (70g), grated finely
¼ cup coarsely chopped fresh flat-leaf parsley
4 pocket pitta breads (340g)
200g sliced roast beef
dressing
2 tablespoons olive oil
2 teaspoons dijon mustard
2 tablespoons white wine vinegar
2 tablespoons water

1 Make dressing.
2 Combine dressing with cabbage, onion, carrot and parsley in medium bowl.
3 Split pitta breads a little more than halfway through; fill pockets with slaw and beef. Wrap in baking paper or plastic wrap.
4 Pack pocket in lunchbox with a freezer brick or frozen drink.
dressing Combine ingredients in screw-top jar; shake well.

preparation time 15 minutes
makes 4
nutritional count per pocket 17.2g total fat (4.2g saturated fat); 1923kJ (460 cal); 48.1g carbohydrate; 25.3g protein; 5.3g fibre

mediterranean tuna baguette

1 medium potato (200g), chopped
1 tablespoon finely chopped black olives
1 medium tomato (150g), seeded, chopped finely
185g can tuna in springwater, drained, flaked
2 small french bread sticks (300g), halved crossways then split in half
30g mesclun
2 hard-boiled eggs, sliced thickly
dressing
2 tablespoons olive oil
1 tablespoon red wine vinegar
1 teaspoon dijon mustard

1 Boil, steam or microwave potato until tender; drain, cool.
2 Make dressing.
3 Combine potato and dressing with olives, tomato and tuna in medium bowl; cover with plastic wrap, refrigerate.
4 The next day, sandwich mesclun, tuna mixture and eggs between roll; Wrap in baking paper or plastic wrap.
5 Pack baguette in lunchbox with a freezer brick or frozen drink.
dressing Combine ingredients in screw-top jar; shake well.

preparation time 15 minutes
cooking time 15 minutes
makes 4
nutritional count per baguette 15.7g total fat (2.9g saturated fat); 1781kJ (426 cal); 47.9g carbohydrate; 20.9g protein; 4.2g fibre

the night before
Boil the eggs and prepare
the filling and dressing;
keep, covered, in the
refrigerator. Assemble the
baguette in the morning.

the night before
The rolls are best
made in the morning.

vietnamese-style
chicken rolls

2 crusty bread rolls (300g)
2 tablespoons mayonnaise
1 cup (160g) shredded barbecued chicken
1 small carrot (70g), grated
½ cup (30g) shredded iceberg lettuce
1 tablespoon sweet chilli sauce
8 fresh coriander leaves

1 Split rolls in half; spread with mayonnaise. Fill with chicken, carrot and lettuce. Drizzle with sauce and top with coriander. Wrap in baking paper or plastic wrap.
2 Pack roll in lunchbox with a freezer brick or frozen drink.

preparation time 5 minutes
makes 2
nutritional count per baguette 18.2g total fat (3.2g saturated fat); 2784kJ (666 cal); 87g carbohydrate; 33.8g protein; 7.3g fibre

cheese, corn & bacon muffins

½ cup (85g) polenta
½ cup (125ml) milk
3 rindless bacon rashers
   (195g), chopped finely
4 green onions, chopped finely
2 eggs, beaten lightly
60g butter, melted
125g can creamed corn
310g can corn kernels, drained
1½ cups (225g) self-raising
   flour
50g cheddar cheese, cut
   into 12 cubes
¼ cup (30g) finely grated
   cheddar cheese

1 Combine polenta and milk in large bowl; stand 10 minutes.

2 Preheat oven to 200°C/180°C fan-forced. Oil 12-hole (⅓-cup/80ml) muffin pan.

3 Cook bacon in heated oiled small frying pan until browned and crisp. Add onion; cook, stirring, 1 minute.

4 Add egg, butter and both corns to polenta mixture; whisk to combine. Add bacon mixture and sifted flour; stir until just combined.

5 Spoon 1 tablespoon muffin mixture into each pan hole; top with a cube of cheese. Divide remaining muffin mixture among pan holes; sprinkle with grated cheese. Bake about 20 minutes. Stand muffins 5 minutes before turning, top-side up, onto a wire rack to cool. Store cold muffins in an airtight container, for up to two days, in the refrigerator.

6 The next day, wrap the muffin in baking paper; pack in lunchbox with a freezer brick or frozen drink.

preparation time 15 minutes
cooking time 25 minutes
makes 12
nutritional count per muffin 9.5g total fat (5.2g saturated fat); 845kJ (226 cal); 24.2g carbohydrate; 9.8g protein; 1.9g fibre

tips Instant polenta is not suitable for this recipe.
the night before Make muffins and keep, covered, in the refrigerator.

the night before
Make rice cakes
and keep, covered,
in the refrigerator.

cheesy spinach rice cakes

½ cup (40g) finely grated parmesan cheese
250g packet frozen chopped spinach, thawed
250g packet pre-cooked white rice
3 eggs, beaten lightly
250g cottage cheese
125g fetta cheese, crumbled
3 green onions, chopped finely

1 Preheat oven to 180°C/160°C fan-forced. Grease 10 holes of a 12-hole (⅓ cup/80ml) muffin pan. Sprinkle base and side of pan holes with half the parmesan cheese.

2 Squeeze excess water from spinach. Combine spinach, rice, egg, cottage cheese, fetta and onion in a large bowl; mix well.

3 Spoon spinach mixture into prepared pan holes. Sprinkle tops with remaining parmesan. Bake about 30 minutes or until browned and just set. Stand cakes 5 minutes before turning, top-side up, onto a wire rack to cool. Store cold cakes in an airtight container, for up to two days, in the refrigerator.

4 The next day, wrap cake in baking paper; pack in lunchbox with a freezer brick or frozen drink.

preparation time 10 minutes
cooking time 30 minutes
makes 10
nutritional count per cake 7.4g total fat (4.2g saturated fat); 594kJ (142 cal); 7.9g carbohydrate; 10.6g protein; 0.9g fibre

asparagus frittata with rocket

cooking-oil spray
1 small red onion (100g),
    sliced thinly
170g asparagus, trimmed,
    cut into 2cm lengths
2 eggs
2 egg whites
2 tablespoons low-fat
    cottage cheese
40g baby rocket leaves
2 tablespoons lemon juice
2 teaspoons drained baby
    capers, rinsed

1 Preheat grill.

2 Spray small frying pan with cooking oil; cook onion over heat, stirring, 1 minute. Add asparagus; cook, stirring, 2 minutes.

3 Meanwhile, combine eggs, egg whites and cheese in a medium jug. Pour over asparagus mixture in pan. Cook, uncovered, 5 minutes or until frittata is browned underneath.

4 Place pan under grill for about 5 minutes or until frittata is set. Cool; cover then refrigerate.

5 The next day, cut frittata into quarters; wrap in baking paper or plastic wrap. Combine remaining ingredients in medium bowl, then place in an airtight plastic container. Pack frittata and salad in lunchbox with a freezer brick or frozen drink.

preparation time 10 minutes
cooking time 15 minutes **serves** 2
nutritional count per serving 6.3g total fat (1.8g saturated fat); 614kJ (147 cal); 5.4g carbohydrate; 16.3g protein; 1.9g fibre
tip If the handle of your frying pan is not heatproof, cover it with aluminium foil before placing it under the grill.

the night before
Make the frittata and keep, covered, in the refrigerator. The salad is best made in the morning.

the night before
Make the slice and
keep, covered, in
the refrigerator.

tomato, zucchini & oregano slice

125g cherry tomatoes
1 egg
3 egg whites
⅓ cup (65g) low-fat cottage cheese
1 clove garlic, crushed
1 small zucchini (90g), grated coarsely
2 tablespoons coarsely chopped fresh oregano leaves
30g baby spinach leaves

1 Preheat oven to 200°C/180°C fan-forced. Line 8cm x 21cm loaf pan with a strip of baking paper.
2 Place tomatoes in prepared pan. Roast 10 minutes.
3 Meanwhile, combine egg, egg whites, cheese and garlic in medium jug.
4 Remove tomatoes from oven; reduce oven temperature to 160°C/140°C fan-forced.
5 Sprinkle tomatoes with zucchini and oregano; pour over egg mixture. Bake about 25 minutes or until set. Cool; cover then refrigerate.
6 The next day, cut slice in half, wrap in baking paper or plastic wrap. Pack spinach in an airtight plastic container. Pack slice and spinach in lunchbox with a freezer brick or frozen drink.

preparation time 10 minutes
cooking time 35 minutes
serves 2
nutritional count per serving 3.3g total fat (1.1g saturated fat); 456kJ (109 cal); 3.1g carbohydrate; 15.7g protein; 2.1g fibre

glossary

bacon rashers also known as slices of bacon.

basil an aromatic herb; there are many types, but the most commonly used is sweet, or common, basil.

beans

butter also known as lima beans; large, flat, kidney-shaped bean, off-white in colour, with a mealy texture and mild taste. Available canned and dried.

green also known as french or string beans (although the tough string they once had has generally been bred out of them), this long thin fresh bean is consumed in its entirety once cooked.

bread

french stick french bread that's been formed into a long, narrow cylindrical loaf. It usually has a crisp brown crust and light chewy interior. A standard stick is 5cm-6cm wide and 3cm-4cm tall, but they can be up to a meter in length. Also known as a french bread, french loaf or baguette.

lavash flat, unleavened bread of Mediterranean origin.

mountain bread wraps a thin, dry, soft-textured flat bread. Available from health food stores and most supermarkets.

pitta also known as lebanese bread. Sold in large, flat pieces that separate into two thin rounds. Also available in small thick pieces called pocket pitta.

butter use salted or unsalted (sweet) butter; 125g is equal to one stick of butter.

button mushrooms small, cultivated white mushrooms having a subtle flavour.

capers the grey-green buds of a warm climate (usually Mediterranean) shrub, sold either dried and salted or pickled in a vinegar brine. Baby capers, those picked early, are smaller, fuller-flavoured and more expensive than the full-sized ones. Capers should be rinsed well before using.

capsicum also known as bell pepper or, simply, pepper. Discard membranes and seeds before use. Also available roasted, packed in water or oil.

cheese

cheddar the most widely eaten cheese in the world, cheddar is a semi-hard cows-milk cheese. It ranges in colour from white to pale yellow, and has a slightly crumbly texture if properly matured. It's aged for between nine months and two years, and the flavour becomes sharper with time.

cottage a fresh, white, unripened curd cheese with a grainy consistency and a fat content of between 5% and 15%.

cream cheese, spreadable light a light version of Philadelphia, a blend of cottage and cream cheeses with a fat content of 21%.

fetta Greek in origin; this crumbly goat- or sheep-milk cheese has a sharp salty taste. It is ripened and stored in a salted whey.

parmesan also known as parmigiano; is a hard, grainy cows-milk cheese. The curd for this cheese is salted in brine for a month before being aged for up to two years in humid conditions.

ricotta the name for this soft, white, cows-milk cheese roughly translates as cooked again. It's made from whey, a by-product of other cheese-making, to which fresh milk and acid are added. Ricotta is a sweet, moist cheese with a fat content of around 8.5% and a slightly grainy texture.

coriander leaves also known as pak chee, cilantro or chinese parsley; a bright-green leafy herb with a pungent flavour.

cucumber lebanese short, slender and thin-skinned. Probably the most popular variety because of its tender, edible skin, tiny, yielding seeds, and sweet, fresh and flavoursome taste.

flour, self-raising a plain (all-purpose) flour sifted with baking powder in the proportion of 1 cup flour to 2 teaspoons baking powder.

ginger, fresh also known as green or root ginger; the thick root of a tropical plant.

lettuce

cos also known as romaine lettuce; the traditional caesar salad lettuce. Long, with leaves ranging from dark green on the outside to almost white near the core; the leaves have a stiff centre rib that gives a slight cupping effect to the leaf on either side.

iceberg a heavy, firm round lettuce with tightly packed leaves and crisp texture.

mesclun also called salad mix or gourmet salad mix; an assorted mix of young lettuce and other green leaves, including curly endive baby spinach and mizuna.

mustard

dijon also known as french. Pale brown, creamy, distinctively flavoured, fairly mild french mustard.

wholegrain also known as seeded. A french-style coarse-grain mustard made from crushed mustard seeds and dijon-style mustard.

noodles, bean thread also known as wun sen, glass or cellophane noodles because they are transparent when cooked. Made from mung bean paste; white in colour, and very delicate; available, dried, in different-sized bundles. Soak before use, unless deep-frying, which requires no pre-soaking.

oil

cooking-oil spray we use a cholesterol-free cooking spray made from canola oil.

olive made from ripened olives. Extra virgin and virgin are the best, while extra light or light refers to taste not fat levels.

peanut pressed from ground peanuts; most commonly used oil in Asian cooking because of its high smoke point (capacity to handle high heat without burning).

vegetable sourced from plants rather than animal fats.

onion

green also known as scallion or, incorrectly, shallot; an immature onion picked before the bulb has formed, having a long, bright-green edible stalk.

red also known as spanish, red spanish or bermuda onion; a sweet-flavoured, large, purple-red onion.

parsley, flat-leaf known as continental or italian parsley.

pastrami the word is derived from the Romanian word "pastra", which means "to preserve". Is a highly seasoned preserved meat usually made from beef. Available from delicatessens.

polenta also known as cornmeal; a flour-like cereal made of dried corn (maize) and sold ground in different textures. Also the name of the dish made from it.

rice, pre-cooked milled, cooked then dried rice. Precooked rice is more porous, so that steam can penetrate the grain and rehydrate it in a short time.

sauces

soy, japanese all-purpose low-sodium soy sauce made with more wheat content than its Chinese counterparts. Possibly the best table soy and the one to choose if you only want one variety. Available in major supermarkets and all Asian food stores.

sweet chilli a comparatively mild, thai-type sauce made from red chillies, sugar, garlic and vinegar.

teriyaki made from soy sauce, mirin, sugar, ginger and other spices; it imparts a distinctive glaze when brushed on grilled meat.

snow pea sprouts tender new growths of snow peas; also known as mange tout.

spinach leaves also known as english spinach and incorrectly, silver beet.

vinegar

cider (apple cider) made from fermented apples.

red wine based on fermented red wine.

rice a colourless vinegar made from fermented rice and flavoured with sugar and salt. Also known as seasoned rice vinegar.

white wine made from a blend of white wines.

wombok also known as peking cabbage, chinese cabbage or petsai. Elongated in shape with pale green crinkly leaves.

zucchini also known as courgette.

conversion chart

MEASURES

One Australian metric measuring cup holds approximately 250ml, one Australian metric tablespoon holds 20ml, one Australian metric teaspoon holds 5ml.

The difference between one country's measuring cups and another's is within a 2- or 3-teaspoon variance, and will not affect your cooking results. North America, New Zealand and the United Kingdom use a 15ml tablespoon. All cup and spoon measurements are level. The most accurate way of measuring dry ingredients is to weigh them. When measuring liquids, use a clear glass or plastic jug with metric markings.

We use large eggs with an average weight of 60g.

DRY MEASURES

METRIC	IMPERIAL
15g	½oz
30g	1oz
60g	2oz
90g	3oz
125g	4oz (¼lb)
155g	5oz
185g	6oz
220g	7oz
250g	8oz (½lb)
280g	9oz
315g	10oz
345g	11oz
375g	12oz (¾lb)
410g	13oz
440g	14oz
470g	15oz
500g	16oz (1lb)
750g	24oz (1½lb)
1kg	32oz (2lb)

LIQUID MEASURES

METRIC	IMPERIAL
30ml	1 fluid oz
60ml	2 fluid oz
100ml	3 fluid oz
125ml	4 fluid oz
150ml	5 fluid oz (¼ pint/1 gill)
190ml	6 fluid oz
250ml	8 fluid oz
300ml	10 fluid oz (½ pint)
500ml	16 fluid oz
600ml	20 fluid oz (1 pint)
1000ml (1 litre)	1¾ pints

LENGTH MEASURES

METRIC	IMPERIAL
3mm	⅛in
6mm	¼in
1cm	½in
2cm	¾in
2.5cm	1in
5cm	2in
6cm	2½in
8cm	3in
10cm	4in
13cm	5in
15cm	6in
18cm	7in
20cm	8in
23cm	9in
25cm	10in
28cm	11in
30cm	12in (1ft)

OVEN TEMPERATURES

These oven temperatures are only a guide for conventional ovens. For fan-forced ovens, check the manufacturer's manual.

	°C (CELSIUS)	°F (FAHRENHEIT)	GAS MARK
Very slow	120	250	½
Slow	150	275-300	1-2
Moderately slow	160	325	3
Moderate	180	350-375	4-5
Moderately hot	200	400	6
Hot	220	425-450	7-8
Very hot	240	475	9

index

TEST KITCHEN
Food director Pamela Clark
Recipe editor Louise Patniotis
Nutritional information Belinda Farlow

ACP BOOKS
General manager Christine Whiston
Editorial director Susan Tomnay
Creative director Hieu Chi Nguyen
Designer Hannah Blackmore
Senior editor Wendy Bryant
Director of sales Brian Cearnes
Marketing manager Bridget Cody
Business analyst Rebecca Varela
Operations manager David Scotto
Production manager Victoria Jefferys
International rights enquiries Laura Bamford
lbamford@acpuk.com

ACP Books are published by ACP Magazines
a division of PBL Media Pty Limited
Publishing director, Women's lifestyle Pat Ingram
Director of sales, Women's lifestyle Lynette Phillips
Commercial manager, Women's lifestyle Seymour Cohen
Marketing director, Women's lifestyle Matthew Dominello
Public relations manager, Women's lifestyle Hannah Deveraux
Creative director, Events, Women's lifestyle Luke Bonnano
Research Director, Women's lifestyle Justin Stone
PBL Media, Chief Executive Officer Ian Law

Cover Traffic light pasta salad, page 15
Photographer Alan Benson
Stylist Marie Hélène Clauzon
Produced by ACP Books, Sydney.

Published by ACP Books,
a division of ACP Magazines Ltd,
54 Park St, Sydney; GPO Box 4088,
Sydney, NSW 2001
phone (02) 9282 8618 fax (02) 9267 9438.
acpbooks@acpmagazines.com.au
www.acpbooks.com.au
Printed by Dai Nippon in Korea.
Australia Distributed by Network Services,
phone +61 2 9282 8777 fax +61 2 9264 3278
networkweb@networkservicescompany.com.au
United Kingdom Distributed by Australian
Consolidated Press (UK),
phone (01604) 642 200 fax (01604) 642 300
books@acpuk.com
New Zealand Distributed by Netlink Distribution
Company, phone (9) 366 9966 ask@ndc.co.nz
South Africa Distributed by PSD Promotions,
phone (27 11) 392 6065/6/7 fax (27 11) 392
6079/80 orders@psdprom.co.za
Canada Distributed by Publishers Group Canada
phone (800) 663 5714 fax (800) 565 3770
service@raincoast.com

Title: Kid's lunches / food director
Pamela Clark.
ISBN: 9781863968522 (pbk.)
Notes: Includes index.
Series: The working mum series
Subjects: Lunchbox cookery.
School children – Food. Children – Nutrition.
Other Authors/Contributors: Clark, Pamela.
Australian women's weekly.
Dewey Number: 641.53
© ACP Magazines Ltd 2009
ABN 18 053 273 546
This publication is copyright. No part of it may be
reproduced or transmitted in any form without
the written permission of the publishers.
Send recipe enquiries to:
recipeenquiries@acpmagazines.com.au